I PROMISE TO BUILD PEOPLE UP!

Written By: Stevon Lester

Illustrated by Eminence System

MW01172387

I Promise To Build People Up!

Copyright © 2024 by Stevon M. Lester LLC

www.Iamstevonlester.com

First Edition

ISBN 979-8-218-55031-8

Written By Stevon Lester

Illustrations by Eminence System

This book is dedicated to my mother and my little sister Jordyn who helped me bring this book to life.

This book belongs to:

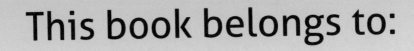

Hi! I'm Stevon. Did you know, that people are more likely to remember the bad things that someone says about them more than the good things that someone has said to them?

What you say about someone has the ability to make them feel really good about themselves or very bad.

You have the power to build people up or tear them down with your words.

In the second grade, my teacher got really mad at me. I was joking around in class with friends when she looked at me and yelled, "Stevon, if you keep acting like this, you will end up homeless!"

Her words hurt me a lot. The class went quiet, and everyone stared at me. It felt like a punch in my chest, and I wanted to cry, but I didn't want everyone to bully me.

I took a deep breath. My lungs felt like they were on fire. I was mad and scared.

I thought, "What if she's right? What if I was going to end up homeless? What if I could never become successful?"

I couldn't stop thinking about what she said. I began to think I wasn't smart, not good at school, and couldn't do anything right. These thoughts stayed with me for a long, long time.

At the time, my teacher didn't realize it but she had used her words to tear me down rather than using them in a positive way to build me up.

Her words changed how I behaved in school. I began to be a bad friend and very mean to people around me.

Before I knew it, I started to use my words to tear other people down instead of building them up. I made fun of the way people looked, the way people dressed, and the way they talked.

Because someone hurt me, I decided to hurt other people with my words. But that wasn't the right thing to do.

As I got older, I continued to get in trouble at school even though I was a nice person on the inside. That was until one day, my teachers in middle school decided to do something different. They decided to give me a nickname!

In middle school, Mrs. Clark said to me, "Stevon, you're smart. You're wise for a kid." She laughed and said, "I will call you Grandpa!"

Grandpa??? I was so confused and embarrassed !

"Yes, Grandpa. Not because of the way you dress or because of the way you talk. We are going to call you grandpa because you are a lot wiser than your age. You just make bad decisions sometimes. We are going to use that nickname to build you up and not tear you down!"

" Wow," I exclaimed. My frown quickly turned into a smile. Finally someone had decided to say something nice about me! I learned that day that my mistakes don't make me. The same way one teacher had a bad moment to use her words to tear me down, another teacher decided to use her words to build me up!

At first, I thought she was making fun of me. But other teachers and students started calling me "Grandpa" too everyday. I liked the new name. They saw me as wise and thoughtful. This changed me. I felt proud of myself. "Hello to the new me! Aka 'Mr. Grandpa!"

Their words allowed me to view myself in a different way, I no longer started to use my words to tear other people down because someone hurt me. But instead I used it as an opportunity to build up other people around me!

Everyday, I found a way to build someone up with my words at my school! I realized that bullying others wasn't the way to go but instead using my words to help others made me become a better person.

Now, I am a motivational speaker. I teach kids about the power of words all across the nation! I share my story with students like you to know that just because someone has said something bad about you doesn't mean you have to say something bad about someone else!

Did you know people forget good things you say but remember bad ones?

We hear so many bad things that our brain often focuses on what's wrong. Sometimes when you look in the mirror you may begin to see things you don't like about yourself. Once you start, it can be hard to stop and think of good things.

In this book, I want to show you that words matter. Your heart hears every negative word you say about others and yourself. But what if we decided to say positive things instead?

What if you said something nice about yourself? What if you didn't join in when others are being mean? What if you made sure people felt better after talking to you?

Guess how much it costs to say something nice to someone else? Absolutely nothing! It's free, you can do it all day every day. However, it may not cost you any money to say something mean to someone else but it can cost them their confidence, a friendship, and much more.

Lesson #3
It's hard to remember all of the good things that someone says about you, but it's easy to remember the rude things. Why is that? Imagine how many people we can help if we decided to build people up with our words instead of tearing them down.

Remember this, just because someone has said something bad to tear someone else down doesn't mean they're a bad person. They might have had a bad moment which is why it's important to forgive!

We have all made mistakes and probably have said something in the past to tear someone else down. However, we can start fresh today!

It starts with a simple promise, the People Builder Decree! Feel free to say this with us.

Say this loud and proud! " I promise to use my words for good. I promise to use my words to build people up and not tear them down. I promise to be the best version of myself and if I do make a mistake I will forgive myself and others!"

We believe in you. Will you
believe in yourself too?

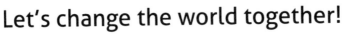

Let's change the world together!

Made in the USA
Columbia, SC
03 December 2024

47055734R00022